On The Edge Of Beautiful

Poems of Love, Life, and the In-Between

Ayush Pradhan

BookLeaf Publishing

India | USA | UK

Made with ❤ on the BookLeaf Publishing Platform
www.bookleafpub.in
www.bookleafpub.com

Dedication

To the ones who dared to dream in the dark, who stumbled and rose, who loved and lost and loved again. To those who find the extraordinary in the ordinary, the beautiful in the broken. This is for you.

Preface

Alright, let's be honest. This book isn't your typical, stuffy poetry collection. It's more like a mixtape of my brain – the thoughts that keep me up at night, the feelings I can't quite explain, and the moments when life feels both beautifully chaotic and strangely profound.

Writing these poems has been my way of untangling the knots in my head, like trying to solve a Rubik's Cube made of emotions. It's been my therapy, my escape, and my way of finding the extraordinary in the 'blah.'

So, welcome to my world, where paradoxes reign, dreams collide with reality, and vulnerability is a superpower. I invite you to flip through these pages, find your own reflections, and maybe, just maybe, realize we're all a little bit 'on the edge of beautiful' in our own perfectly imperfect ways.

Acknowledgements

This book? It's basically a team effort. Big thanks to my family and friends, who, despite witnessing my transformation into a slightly eccentric poet, still managed to love and support me. You're the best.

To all the poets and writers who came before me: you dropped the mic, and I'm just here trying to pick it up and not drop it myself. Your words have been my fuel, my fire, and my 'Wait, I wish I'd written that!' moments.

And to her – you know who you are. Thanks for showing up and inspiring the chaos in my head to turn into something resembling art. You're pretty awesome.

And to you, reader: thanks for taking a chance on my little book of feelings. Writing is how I untangle my brain, process life's curveballs, and try to find the funny side of it all. These poems are my therapy, and sharing it is my way of saying, 'Hey, we're all in this together, right? I hope you enjoy the ride, maybe find a piece of yourself in these pages, and remember that life, like a good poem, is best enjoyed with a bit of heart and a dash of humor.

Section 1 : Figuring Myself Out

Ever felt like you're looking in the mirror and wondering who's staring back? Yeah, me too. These poems are all about digging deep, embracing the quirks, and figuring out this whole identity thing.

1. **The Mirror and I:** This one's about loving all of it, even the messy parts.
2. **Be Real:** Screw the filters, let's just be ourselves, yeah?
3. **Paradox:** Life's full of contradictions, and that's okay.
4. **The Delusional Blueprint:** Dream big, even if people think you're crazy.
5. **True Beauty:** It's not about what's on the outside, it's about what's within.
6. **Maturity in progress:** Growing up is a journey, not a destination.

1. The Mirror and I

How can I not love this body I wear,
This patchwork of scars and starlight?
It has carried me through every storm,
A silent warrior, unseen by the night.

The heart—it beats without applause,
No audience to cheer its silent fight.
But oh, it has held oceans of grief,
And still dared to seek the morning light.

These legs have climbed the mountains I chose,
And stumbled when the world was steep.
These eyes have wept, but oh, they've seen,
The beauty that life hides in deep.

Every wrinkle, every scar, every bruise,
A map of where I've been, who I've fought to be.
Do I wish them erased? Not a single one,
For they are the ink of my history.

Who else has heard the wars in my head,
And still whispered, "We will survive"!
Who else has sat with me in the dark,
And lit the match to keep me alive?

How can I not love the only one,
Who has never left my side?
Through solitude, chaos, and fleeting joy,
I have always been my guide.

2. Paradox

Be a paradox, don't fit the mold,
Get jacked, stay sharp, let your story unfold.
Lift those weights, and then lift your mind,
Read a few books, leave the limits behind.

Be a beast at work, go savage, go hard,
But find your peace in your own backyard.
Walk like a champ, head held high,
Yet work like an underdog—reach for the sky.

Don't let the world box you in tight,
It's your game to play, your light to ignite.
Societal norms? They're just smoke and mirrors
Fit in too well, and you'll vanish, my dear

Like Tetris blocks, those that blend disappear,
But the ones who stand out are the ones we revere.
So stick to the grind, be bold, stand tall
The world opens up when you refuse to fall.

3. Be Real

Be you—it's what they all say,
But it's tough when the world pulls you away.
"Say this, do that, walk this way,"
You wonder if you'll ever have a say.

But who wrote these rules? Who made the call?
Why fit into boxes that feel so small?
You've got your own story, your own wild song,
Why let someone else tell you it's wrong?

Some will cheer, and some will doubt,
Some will leave, and some will shout.
But the ones who matter, they'll stick around,
They'll love your edges, not just what's round.

So laugh too hard, cry when you feel,
Say what you mean, and let yourself heal.
Life's not a script, there's no perfect way—
Just be you, every single day.

4. The Delusional Blueprint

They say I built castles in clouds too thin,
wrote symphonies on the edge of the wind,
mapped roads through oceans no one could see,
and sketched constellations where stars shouldn't be.

"Delusional," they whisper, with pity or pride,
as I wrestle with shadows and call it a guide.
But what is a boundary but someone's design,
a line they mistook for the end of the line?

What if the sky was just earth upside down?
What if the mountain was tired of the ground?
What if the stars are mirrors, not light,
Reflecting the dreams we leave in the night?

I plant my mistakes like seeds in the dirt,
watch them grow wild through chaos and hurt.
Each crack in my logic is water, not shame—
a river that carries my fears into flame.

So call me unhinged, a bit out of sync,
But I'll toast to the crazy before I rethink.
For genius is reckless, a child of surprise,
And the universe bends to the daring and wise.

Here's to the audacious, the dreamers who leap,
Who wager their souls on promises deep.
Give me delusion, a stage, and a pen—
I'll carve the impossible, again and again.

5. True Beauty

Beauty, they say, isn't earned by toil,
It's a gift that parents pass down, like soil.
The glow of youth, it flickers and flows,
Like petals on roses, sags as it grows.

No work of your own, yet the pride's on full blast,
They walk with a swagger, thinking it'll last.
But sunlight, my dear, can melt that glow,
Leaving behind what you never did know.

Now, real beauty, my friend, is a different game,
It's not in the mirror or your Instagram fame.
It's in the way you think, the wisdom you share,
In the way you laugh, without a single care.

When I look at you, I see much more,
Than just a face that others adore.
Your kindness is sharper than your witty line,
And that, my dear, is where you truly shine.

Your mind's a circus, full of fun and surprise,
A place where thoughts do somersaults and highs.
You've got a grace that's far from cliché,
A beauty that's quirky, in every way.

So while others may chase what time will erase,
I find true beauty in your gentle grace.
For you are the one who makes life fun,
A beauty that's endless, like a well-timed pun.

6. Maturity in progress

Maturity is what you call 'quiet strength',
The calm that rises when storms are near,
It's standing firm in what you feel,
Yet open to what others reveal.

It's not in years or battles fought,
But in the way you handle thought.
A clash of words yet no need to fight,
It's about knowing you can't be always right.

For sometimes being kind and still,
Is not just bending to others' will.
But knowing when to speak or stand,
With grace, not force or heavy hand.

Sometimes being immature is wise,
Like when you laugh, and don't disguise
The simple joy of being free,
A playful heart can help you see.

Immaturity, at times, can show
What strict maturity won't know
That letting go, and being light,
Can be just as wise as being right.

It's knowing life's not always straight,
That fun and joy can't always wait.
Maturity knows when to be free,
And immaturity shows us how to be.

Section 2 : Love - The Rollercoaster

Okay, let's talk about love. It's messy, it's exhilarating, it's heartbreaking, and it's oh-so-beautiful. These poems capture the ups and downs, the what-ifs, and the forever-hopes.

1. **Those Eyes:** That moment when you lock eyes with someone and the world just stops.
2. **The Way You Feel:** Feeling all the feels, the good, the bad, and the in-between.
3. **"Fall" in love:** Taking that leap of faith, even if it scares the hell out of you.
4. **The Math of Love:** Love doesn't always add up, but that's part of the mystery.
5. **A Soliloquy of Love:** When love is a one-way street, but your heart still sings.
6. **The One who waits:** That ache in your soul for someone who might not feel the same.
7. **Lost and Found:** Finding your home in another person's heart.

8. **Stronger still:** Picking up the pieces and coming back even stronger.

9. **To you:** A love letter to the one who makes your soul sing.

10. **Independent Queen for dummies:** They're amazing, but they can be confusing.

1. Those Eyes

Between black and white, there's shade of grey,
But between life and death, your brownish eyes stay.
They speak of moments, neither lost or found,
Whispered truths that never make a sound.

They hold the dawn of hope and dusk of dreams,
A silent world of thoughts, or so it seems.
Between every heartbeat and every sigh,
They hold the answer to the endless why.

Like twilight between day and dark,
They leave on the soul a quiet mark.
Where mystery and truth collides,
In those brown eyes my world resides.

2. The Way You Feel

You love like the ocean meets the shore,
As if each wave is begging for more.
Every heartbeat is a final call,
To give everything, or nothing at all.

You feel too much, like a comet's flight,
Briefly seen, but it reshapes the night.
Where joy dances like sparks on a flame,
Yet pain carves stories without a name.

Did you know trees hum beneath the ground,
Root to root, where no ears can be found?
You feel like that—silent, unseen,
Yet holding the world in what might have been.

But maybe this storm you carry inside,
Is the price of living with eyes open wide.
To love, to break, to feel it all—
Is the bravest gift, and your greatest call

3. "Fall" in love

Love is a fall, one you choose to take,
A little piece of yourself you give and break.
It's the fire in the chest, rushes through your veins,
Weird kind of thrill, that erases the pain.

You know the fall, ground is waiting below,
But still you dive, deep down you just know.
You know the fall will bring you pain,
But somehow, you'd do it all again.

It's not the safety, it's the flight,
You die all-day, can't live all night.
Breathless and burning, yet you can't pull away,
Because love is a risk you choose every day.

4. The Math of Love

Love isn't simple—it never adds clean,
Two different minds, no in-between.
Some days you multiply laughter and light,
Some days you divide just to make things feel right.

It's balancing silence, knowing the cost,
Gaining in moments, but sometimes feeling lost.
It's proof without numbers, no formula clear,
A gamble on trust, a wager on years.

It's solving the riddle of all that they hide,
Reading the lines in the words left aside.
Not knowing the answer, but staying to see,
Not always agreeing, but choosing to be.

Because love isn't logic, it's trial and error,
A beautiful mess, a lifelong endeavor.
Not perfect, not easy, but real in its way
An equation worth solving, day after day.

5. A Soliloquy of Love

I loved you in ways I never knew,
with hands outstretched, yet never two.
Love, I thought, was meant to grow,
but roots won't shake where winds won't blow.

You feared a love that may never grow,
I feared the love you'd never know.
Two souls, side by side, yet miles apart,
one beating freely, one guarding its heart.

Was it love if it stood alone?
A fire unlit, yet fully known?
Or was it merely a wish, a dream,
a river lost to its own stream?

Still, love is love, even unseen,
not owed, not held, yet evergreen.
So I let it rest, not as regret,
but as a story—unheard yet.

6. The One who waits

You feel that love should be soft and sweet,
a dance of hands, two hearts same beat.
Yet here I stand on hollow ground,
where I'm lost and love is found.

You stole my breath, then let me choke,
sold me a dream, then laughed at the smoke.
You lit the match, then watched it die,
called it love—I called it a lie.

I tried to leave, to shift the blame,
to trade my torch for colder flames.
But love is rigged—I play, I lose,
no matter which role I choose.

I play it cool, delay my fate,
pretend that I don't mind the wait.
But love's a clock that bends for two—
it stops for me, runs fast for you.

For love is war without a fight,
a silent storm, a sleepless night.
And if I'm here despite the cost,
then tell me—have I won or lost?

7. Lost and Found

I am the shadow that follows near,
You are the sunlight, vibrant and clear.
Unseen without you, I fade into night,
While you remain the bringer of light.

I am the bookmark, plain and unseen,
You are the book, rich with dreams in between.
A placeholder at best, I mark where you've been,
While you are the pages that pull people in.

I'm the thread in your sweater, holding it tight,
You're the warmth it brings on a cold, quiet night.
I'm unseen, forgotten, a stitch in the seam,
You're the comfort that wraps around every dream.

I'm the whistle of the kettle, faint in its song,
You're the tea steeping, rich and strong.
I'm the steam that fades as the moment starts,
You're the sip that soothes and mends weary hearts.

I am the dust in the vastness of space,
Yet in your orbit, I find my place.
I am the drop in the vast, endless sea,
But somehow, the ocean belongs to me.

8. Stronger Still

Some days, you feel like you're always in between,
Someone's comfort, someone's dream.
A shoulder to lean on, a reason to stay,
But love? That never quite comes your way.

You're seen, you're heard, but not too deep,
Left behind when they take their leap.
You wonder where it all went wrong,
When all you wanted was to belong.

Did you dream too big, or love too small?
Was your heart too open, or not at all?
Life feels like a puzzle, a blind race,
Chasing a dream that moves out of place.

You wish you could be someone new,
With different eyes, a different view.
But deep inside, you know what's true,
People like you? You always push through.

You choose kindness, though the world's not fair,
You keep giving, even when no one's there.
You smile, even when your heart's in pain,
And find strength in every drop of rain.

Each fall brings you closer to the end,
Will stronger than time, hard to bend
The tunnel's dark, but you see the light,
And you ain't going down, without a fight.

9. To You

I packed my bags and left the shore,
To find what life was holding in store.
But every city, every street,
Was just a path for us to meet.

For in your eyes, I found my stay,
A place where I would lose my way.
No need to wander, no need to roam,
For in your love, I've found my home.

A place beyond the map I'll find,
Where love has left the world behind.
In every step, in every view,
The journey always leads to you.

10. Independent Queen for dummies

She's the type who stands tall,
Even when life throws her against the wall.
Strength isn't a choice—it's her way of being,
But even the strongest long for freeing

Her life is a fight for every win,
A battle for happiness from deep within.
So when you're with her, remember this:
Softness isn't extra—it's what she'll miss.

Respect Her Boundaries, Give Her Space,
She's not running off—it's her sacred place.
Don't take it as distance; it's where she'll thrive,
Let her recharge and come back alive.

She loves honesty, straight and clear,
No need for games, just stay sincere.
She's seen enough to know what's real,
What matters to her is how you make her feel..

It's the little joys that light her way,
A quiet moment, a thoughtful day.
Challenge her mind, but hear her too,
She's strong, she's wise—and she chose you.

So love her gently, love her well,
Give her room to shine, to rebel.
She's an independent woman, fierce and free,
And with your love, imagine what she could be.

Section 3 : Life's Adventures

Life, man. It's a wild ride. These poems are about navigating the twists and turns, learning from the bumps, and celebrating the victories, big and small.

1. **The First step:** Just start. That's the hardest part, but you got this.
2. **It's Okay:** Messing up is part of the process. Give yourself a break.
3. **Running Away:** Sometimes you need to escape, but eventually, you gotta face the music.
4. **Wings and Rain:** Even in the toughest storms, there's beauty and resilience.
5. **One Step at a Time:** Slow and steady wins the race.
6. **Goodbyes that Stay:** Saying goodbye hurts, but the memories remain.
7. **I see you:** To the ones who feel unseen, you are loved, you are worthy.

1. The First Step

They said I had to take a leap,
To chase the dreams I couldn't keep.
Yet standing there, I felt so small,
Afraid to move, afraid to fall.

Then came a thought, soft and clear,
Just take one step, start right here.
So I moved, though my heart still shook,
A tiny step was all it took.

One step turned into two, then three,
And slowly, the path welcomed me.
I didn't leap, I didn't run,
but step by step, the climb was done.

So take that step, however small,
You'll find it changes after all.
Now looking back, it's clear to see,
The first small step set me free.

2. Its Okay

It's okay if your plans fall apart,
If the map you made doesn't match the start.
It's okay if the script's out of sync,
If life rewrites faster than you can think.

It's okay to feel a little lost,
To count the dreams and weigh the cost.
It's okay to pause, to sit with your fears,
Let them soften with time, not disappear.

It's okay to wander, it's okay to stray—
Trust in yourself; you'll find your way.
It's okay if your life's a sitcom, laugh at the joke,
The chaos is where we all find hope

3. Running Away

Running away, it's what we do,
When problems come, and we don't know what to do.
We run from stress, from fear, from pain
Trying to escape, but it's all in vain

Running away isn't the answer, they say
But it's the only question I ask every day
What else can we do, when troubles surround
Where can I go, everything is upside down

We can't run from our troubles, no matter how hard we
try
They'll always catch up, and we'll wonder why
We didn't face them, and make them go away
Instead we ran, and let them stay

But when you run away, you might just find,
A piece of yourself you left behind.
Once you find yourself, no more need to flee
You'll be as calm as you can be.

Running doesn't always help, some might state
Unless you're chubby, then it's great!
Running away shows who really care
Who'll come find you, who'll be there

So, should you run or should you stay?
Either way, you'll be okay.
Just remember, growth comes from facing the test
And finding yourself is the greatest quest.

4. Wings and Rain

Sometimes we walk the same old road,
Until we choose a lighter load.
We stumble, fall, and make mistakes—
But every bruise is what it takes.

So don't be harsh, don't punish you,
It's all a part of growing through.

Think of the butterfly's gentle way,
Resting her wings on a rainy day.
When storms pass on, she'll rise again,
Bright and free, beyond the pain.

It's okay to rest and take your time,
Your wings will heal, you'll rise, you'll climb.

5. One Step at a Time

Everyone says to show up each day,
To keep grinding, pushing, finding your way.
But they don't tell you how it drains your soul,
How sometimes it takes everything to stay whole.

They tell you to keep moving, don't quit yet,
But not how close you are to the edge you've met.
No one talks about the quiet fight,
The courage it takes to last another night.

"Be kind to yourself," they love to say,
But not how hard it is when you feel in the way.
When your own thoughts turn into a storm,
And being gentle with yourself feels far from the norm.

They talk about self-love like it's easy to do,
But they don't mention the battles inside you.
The doubts, the comparisons, the endless race,
The struggle to find peace in your own space.

So if you're tired and feeling worn thin,
Remember, the strength is within.
Take just one step, one moment, one breath,
You've made it this far — and that's success.

6. Goodbyes that Stay

I've said goodbye a thousand times,
To loves I thought would always be mine.
My childhood home, my first best friend,
A family once whole, now scattered in the wind.

But they all live on in the depths of my heart,
Proof that love doesn't end, it just learns to restart.
They remind me I'm human, I've loved, I've let go,
And found my way through the highs and the low.

The pain felt endless, the nights dragged on,
Yet the sun still rose, and life moved along.
It's funny like that—how time doesn't care,
It heals you in moments you're not even aware.

So here's to loving, losing, and letting go,
to finding joy in what little we know.
That love, once ours, never really ends
it just shifts and grows, and forever ascends.

7. I see you

I see the weight you carry every day,
The silent fight that no one else can know.
You push yourself, believing there's some way,
But sometimes it's okay to just let go.

The world says you should never make mistakes,
And with your every step victory lie,
But in the fall, your inner beast wakes,
And life is lived when you risk to die.

Your flaws and stumbles make you who you are,
They're part of what it means to truly grow.
You've always been enough, you've come so far,
It's time to breathe, relax, and take it slow.

So here's the truth, no need to chase or strive
You're whole, you're seen, you're loved, you are alive.

Section 4 : Deep Thoughts and Realizations

Ever lie awake at night pondering the meaning of life? Yeah, me too. These poems are about the big questions, the inner struggles, and the search for peace.

1. **Faith, Hope and Peace:** Choosing to believe, even when things are tough.
2. **Holding on and Letting go:** Finding that balance between the past and the future.
3. **A Lifetime of Todays:** Living in the moment, 'cause that's all we really have.
4. **Chasing Peace:** Inner peace is the real treasure, not the external stuff.
5. **Strength in Silence:** Sometimes the loudest answers come from the quietest moments.
6. **The shadows we carry:** We all have darkness, but it doesn't define us.
7. **Grace:** Showing kindness, even when it's hard.
8. **Fuel for the Fire:** Turning negativity into motivation.

9. **Living Incognito:** Sometimes the best life is the one lived quietly, authentically.

1. Faith, Hope and Peace

"Is there a meaning to all of this?"
I ask the voice that lives in me.
"If there is, I can't be sure—
But does it help to know completely?"

"But people claim they understand,
Some believe and some deny."
"They believe because they need to,
And doubt because they're scared to try."

"So faith is useless?" I insist.
"Not at all, but it's a choice—
A bridge that leads where facts fall short,
A quiet thought beneath the noise."

"But what if I believe in lies?"
"Then test them well—don't just obey.
Use your mind, but don't ignore
The things your heart still longs to say."

"And when it's over, what comes next?"
"That's one thing neither side can prove.
But if it brings you peace to hope,
Then let that hope be yours to choose."

2. Holding on and Letting go

Hold on to the memories that feel like home,
But let go of the ones that won't leave you alone.
Keep the past close, it shapes who you are,
But release its grip to reach for the stars.

Hold on to your fight when the odds feel unfair,
But let go of battles that lead to despair.
Fight for love when it feels so near,
But let it fly if it's bound by fear.

Anchor your soul in what feels true,
But let the tide take what isn't for you.
Cherish the roots that ground you to stay,
Embrace the winds that pull you away.

Keep the moments that make your heart sing,
Set free the weight of every lost thing
Life's is in balance, a rhythm we know,
A dance of holding on and letting it go.

3. A Lifetime of Todays

When it hurts,
I whisper softly to pain,
"We'll talk tomorrow."
Tomorrow's, a gentle lie,
never arrives,
but it gets me through the night.

Today feels heavy,
but a thread of hope
pulls me forward.
A thread spun from silence,
from promises I don't believe,
but cling to anyway.

And so,
I gather my todays,
stack them high,
a quiet fortress against the storm,
knowing each one survived
is a victory.

Tomorrow may never come,
but today,
I am here.
And somehow,
that is enough.

4. Chasing Peace

If all I desire came true today,
Would peace then come and stay.
But what if hope has a clever disguise,
A sweet illusion, wrapped in lies?

Peace isn't found when life's all right,
You can be hurt, but still feel light.
Miss the past, yet feel it near,
Feeling lost, yet hold no fear.

Peace is not a place I have to find,
In a world full of chaos, lets pray for peace in mind.
Unless I crave an endless sleep,
Or learn to love what's mine to keep.

And when desires have all been met,
Will peace appear? Don't bet just yet.
For us humans always want some more,
Once wishes knock upon our door.

5. Strength in Silence

When someone asks me what I want,
I smile, softly, and say
Everything money can't touch, can't hold, can't claim,
Like laughter that lingers long after the joke,
Like sunlight on the skin, when the day feels too heavy.

I wander to places that humble me,
Mountains so high they drown my thoughts in silence,
Oceans that whisper, "You are small, just like your
problems"
It's funny how the world feels vast enough
To hold all my worries,
And yet, they slip away,
Like sand through open hands.

Hard things stick around, don't they?
Cling to our minds like rain-soaked clothes,
Until one day, they teach us what we were too blind to
see.
Pain becomes a patient teacher,

And we reluctant students
Only learn when we're ready to listen.

The past?
I visit it sometimes,
But I don't unpack.
It's a place to learn from, not to live in,
Like old love letters kept in a drawer
You don't read them every day,
But you know they're there,
Reminding you how far you've come.

And you?
I don't think the storms you faced made you stronger.
No.
They simply showed you
The strength that was already inside,
A quiet force, waiting
To rise.

6. The Shadows We Carry

Behind every person that forgives and heals,
Is a heart that knows how regret feels.
We carry our scars, each one a sign,
Of bravery, mistakes, and borrowed time.

Every soul, no matter how kind,
Has corners of darkness hidden in mind.
Even the bravest hearts have moments they've failed,
Times they've stumbled or their courage bailed.

And every home, no matter how bright,
Has corners where things stay out of sight.
So let's not act like we're perfect or whole,
Our flaws and shadows complete our soul.

7. Grace

When their words cut deep,
or their silence feels like stone,
I've learned it's not my reflection,
in the mirror of their tone.

Their battles rage in shadows,
hidden far from view,
and their storms are not my doing,
they're just passing through.

It's not about my worth,
nor a measure of my place,
it's a weight they bear within,
I'm learning grace.

Grace to step aside,
to not hold on so tight,
to see the hurt in anger
and the fear behind the fight.

For when you know the heart
holds struggles it can't show,
you find a softer way to love—
and let the sorrow go.

8. Fuel for the Fire

They smile, they clap, they stand in the crowd,
but listen closely—jealousy is loud.
A pat on the back, a cheer for the show,
but deep in their hearts, they don't want you to grow.

They liked you better when you were behind,
chasing their footsteps, stuck in the grind.
Now that you're rising, they're shifting their tone,
because your success reminds them of their own.

They won't say they hate you, no, not out loud,
they'll fake their love, blend into the crowd.
A compliment here, a handshake there,
but watch their eyes—they tell you beware.

Let them whisper, let them doubt,
turn their envy inside out.
Hate is just fuel, pour it in,
let it burn and watch you win.

They don't hate you, not really—it's true,
they just hate the fact they can't be you.

9. "Life" at work

Life, work, or both intertwined,
What do we seek, what do we find?
Is it balance, or is it meaning we crave?
In this journey, what do we save?

Balance, they say, is key to it all,
Yet passion may sometimes make us fall.
Success we chase, but with it stress,
Is it worth it, this endless mess?

In this race, we run with no end in sight,
But what's it all for, in the grand light?
When life fades away, what remains of our toil?
Does work define us, or is there more to uncoil?

Beyond the grind, what stories do we hold?
Life's lessons, in tales, often untold.
Does success at work mean life's complete?
Or is there more, beneath our feet?

Work gives purpose, a reason to strive,
But does it overwhelm, as we try to thrive?
Questions linger in a tangled sea,
Is this how work was meant to be?

10. Living Incognito

I'll live my life, all wild and free
Lesser known and wrapped in mystery.
No one asks me what I've done,
So I can mess up just for fun!

When no one knows the road I choose,
There's nothing left for me to lose.
I fail and flop, who's gonna know?
I'll just pretend it's part of the show.

I take my time, I move with ease,
I set the rules, I do as I please.
I live my life, and here's the key—
I'm not famous, but I'm free!

Section 5: Finding the Magic

Life's full of surprises, little moments of wonder that make it all worthwhile. These poems are about appreciating the small stuff and dreaming big.

1. **The Universe in the Small:** Finding the extraordinary in the ordinary.
2. **Little Things:** It's the little things that matter most.
3. **When wishes come true:** Sometimes dreams come true, but it's not always easy.
4. **On the Edge of Beautiful:** That feeling of anticipation, of something amazing just around the corner.

1. The Universe in the Small

To find the sky in a drop of rain,
And the ocean in a tear,
Feel the sun within a single flame,
And the cosmos drawing near.

To hear the wind in a quiet sigh,
And a song in the silence of night,
Hold decades in a passing moment,
And the stars in a blink of light.

The smallest things contain the whole,
The rise, the fall, the vast, the small.
Entire universe within our view,
If only we pause to see it all.

2. Little Things

I want to know the little things that make you, you
The thoughts you have when no one's near,
The dreams you chase, the fears you outgrew,
And how you feel when doubts appear.

I want to hear about your day,
The sunset on your drive back home,
The things you wish you didn't say,
The moments when you feel alone.

The song that plays inside your head,
That's what I really want to know.
The days you wish you stayed in bed,
The little feelings you barely show,

I want to see beyond your grin,
Not just the highs, but every scar,
To understand what lies within,
I want to know you as you are.

3. When wishes Come True

I wished for something, and it came true,
But holding it feels so big, so new.
I thought I'd feel happy, just pure delight,
But now it feels heavy, like I might not do it right.

I asked for the stars, but forgot to see,
That shining so bright comes with a fee.
Will I drop it? Will it fade away?
These fears haunt me every day.

So now I ask for more than blessings,
More than the rush that dreaming brings.
I pray for strength, for steady hands,
For wisdom to meet life's demands.

Because blessings are beautiful, but they need a guide,
Someone who can hold them, not just hide.
So when you dream, dream big, it's true,
But ask for the wisdom to see it through.

4. On the Edge of Beautiful

I like to think I'm always near
To something bright, to something clear.
A flower waiting to unfold,
A quiet dream worth more than gold.

They say my head's too far from ground,
That dreams like mine don't stick around.
But miracles, I've seen them shine,
And I believe the stars do align.

Each prayer, each hope, each silent fight,
Must lead me closer to the light.
No place feels like it's quite my own,
But somewhere waits to be my home.

Adventure whispers, soft and near,
A call that only I can hear.
That someday soon, it all will show—
Why I wandered, why I hoped so.

So I will dream, and I will wait,
For beauty works at its own rate.
I know I'm close—I feel the pull,
On the edge of something beautiful.

Section 6 : Feeling It All

Life's a rollercoaster of emotions, and that's what makes it so damn beautiful. These poems are about embracing the full spectrum, from the highs to the lows.

1. **Happiness Is:** It's not a destination, it's a journey, and it's within you.
2. **Surprise is:** Those unexpected moments that take your breath away.
3. **Anger is:** It's okay to be angry, but don't let it consume you.
4. **Sadness Is:** Sometimes you gotta feel the sadness to appreciate the joy.
5. **Fear is:** It can paralyze you, or it can propel you forward.
6. **Live It All:** Embrace it all, the good, the bad, and the messy. It's all part of the journey.

1. Happiness Is

Happiness isn't gift-wrapped or stored on a shelf,
It's something we make, it's built by ourselves.
It's there in our thoughts, when we're willing to try,
And in each small moment we let anger slide by.

Happiness shines in the purpose we chase,
In the peace of our actions, the smile on our face.
It's laughing at your problems, either big or small,
It's cheering yourself for no reason at all.

Happiness is in jokes, in smiles that stay,
It's in simple things that brighten your day.
Happiness is easy, it's quiet, it's small—
Just let it come, and you'll see it's in all.

2. Surprise is

Surprise is a knock when you thought you'd be alone,
A voice from the past, a laugh on the phone.
It's finding wonder in your daily routine,
Like light falling softly where shadows have been.

Surprise isn't grand, not always loud—
It's quiet, unplanned, hidden in the crowd.
It's buried in corners you thought you knew,
Like a twist in a story that somehow feels true.

Surprise is the twist in a familiar tale,
The warmth of a hug when you thought you'd fail.
Sometimes it's loud, sometimes it's small,
But surprise, at its core, is just life after all.

3. Anger is

Anger's a fire, sometimes a spark,
A flash in the day, a growl in the dark.
It's buried in our chest, tight and deep,
From words held back, secrets we keep.

It's in the breath we hold too long,
When something feels right but turns out wrong.
It's the sting of pride when life feels unfair,
It's knowing you cared when no one else cared.

But anger's a mirror—it shows what we care,
What we protect, what we don't want to share.
Sometimes it fades, clear as a tear,
And shows us a heart that's hiding in fear.

4. Sadness Is

Sadness isn't always in tears that fall,
It's the silence, the void, no sound at all.
It's the ache in your chest, the weight that you bear,
And finding no comfort, though people may care.

It's in moments you hide, in words left unsaid,
In the dreams once alive, now quietly dead.
It's the nights that feels endless, the stars out of sight,
The struggle to find even one bit of light.

Sadness is heavy, it pulls you down slow,
A weight that's familiar, yet hard to let go.
It's trying to smile when you just want to cry,
It's saying "I'm fine" when it's only a lie.

5. Fear is

Fear isn't a monster hiding in night,
It's that cold, quiet feeling when things don't feel right.
It's the rush in your chest, the tremble in your hand,
When you walk somewhere new, or don't understand.

Fear's in the risks, the dreams you don't dare,
It's the voices in the head, "don't fail. Beware."
It's in the things you love, the things you might lose,
In choices that scare you, in paths you can't choose.

It shows us our strength, that we're more than we knew
—
Fear comes to teach us, to help us push through.
When we face it, we grow, our path becomes clear,
And we find that courage is hidden in fear.

6. Live It All

Life isn't a quest to stay happy each day,
It's a dance of emotions in a unexpected way.
It's laughter that echoes, tears that fall,
The thrill of the rise, the fear of the fall.

Don't chase perfection, it doesn't exist,
Feel every feeling, don't let them be missed.
Laugh when it's easy, cry when it's not,
Live through the mess, give it all you've got.

Do it trembling, do it unsure,
Do it heartbroken, searching for cure.
Let new paths guide you, let them reveal,
That even the pain can help you heal.

Life's an adventure, quiet or loud,
A patchwork of moments, both timid and proud.
So live it all, the highs and the lows,
Through every feeling, a new story grows.

Through joy and fear, anger and tears,
I've carried it all, through the quietest years.
Not to escape, but to finally see,
Every emotion is part of me

Section 7 : Work in Progress - Understanding Myself

Ever feel like you're not quite fully formed? Like there's a glitch in your personal matrix? This section is for all those moments. It's the place where my thoughts get a little tangled, my feelings get a little raw, and my understanding of myself takes a detour. It's a 'Work in Progress' because the debugging is still in process. Enter at your own risk (but know that it's a safe space for beautiful imperfections).

1. Strength in Silence

When someone asks me what I want,
I smile, softly, and say
Everything money can't touch, can't hold, can't claim,
Like laughter that lingers long after the joke,
Like sunlight on the skin, when the day feels too heavy.

I wander to places that humble me,
Mountains so high they drown my thoughts in silence,
Oceans that whisper, "You are small, just like your
problems"
It's funny how the world feels vast enough
To hold all my worries,
And yet, they slip away,
Like sand through open hands.

Hard things stick around, don't they?
Cling to our minds like rain-soaked clothes,
Until one day, they teach us what we were too blind to
see.
Pain becomes a patient teacher,

And we reluctant students
Only learn when we're ready to listen.

The past?
I visit it sometimes,
But I don't unpack.
It's a place to learn from, not to live in,
Like old love letters kept in a drawer
You don't read them every day,
But you know they're there,
Reminding you how far you've come.

And you?
I don't think the storms you faced made you stronger.
No.
They simply showed you
The strength that was already inside,
A quiet force, waiting
To rise.

2. A Lifetime of Todays

When it hurts,
I whisper softly to pain,
"We'll talk tomorrow."
Tomorrow's, a gentle lie,
never arrives,
but it gets me through the night.

Today feels heavy,
but a thread of hope
pulls me forward.
A thread spun from silence,
from promises I don't believe,
but cling to anyway.

And so,
I gather my todays,
stack them high,
a quiet fortress against the storm,
knowing each one survived
is a victory.

Tomorrow may never come,
but today,
I am here.
And somehow,
that is enough.

3. Love and Fear

Do you ever sit with fear,
like an old friend who visits unannounced,
pulling up a chair in the quietest corner of your mind?
It doesn't shout, it doesn't beg—
it lingers, a shadow stretching
from the light and warmth of something you love too
much to lose.

Fear and love, they stay together,
partners on a stage you didn't know you built.
One steps forward, the other pulls back,
a rhythm as old as time.
Fear whispers, "What if it all falls apart?"
And love, in its quiet defiance, answers,
"But what if it all comes together?"

I used to think fear was an enemy,
an intruder breaking into my peace.
But fear is not the thief—it's the guard at the gate,
standing watch over the things that matter most.

Where it lingers, purpose hides,
wrapped in layers of discomfort,
waiting for the brave to unravel it.

And love?
Love is the seed we bury in trembling hands,
And hope is what we water it with a cautious faith.
It asks us to wait, to trust,
to believe in the fruit we've yet to taste.

Sometimes, I wonder if the mountain knows the echo,
if it feels the weight of the voice calling back to it.
Perhaps fear is the echo—
a response to the love we send into the void,
returning only to remind us
that we cared enough to call out in the first place.

So, my friend, don't run from fear.
Sit with it. Hold its hand.
Ask it what it guards,
what treasure it stands before.
And when you feel its weight,
remember:
Fear calls us to rise,
and love gives us the reason.

4. Anxiety, The Ghost I know

It knocks like a friend but enters like fear,
a voice in my head that I have to hear.
It sits at my table, it lingers nearby,
it never says hello—but it never says goodbye.

It turns rest into waiting, joy into doubt,
makes me second-guess what I can't live without.
It speaks in my voice, it thinks in my mind,
rewrites every story with danger behind.

It makes me rehearse what I'll never say,
replay mistakes from years away.
It tells me to fix what no one recalls,
to answer questions that never were asked at all.

It steals my hunger, it steals my sleep,
turns empty rooms into secrets to keep.
It makes the quiet feel too loud,
and lonely streets feel like a crowd.

But I've learned its tricks, I know its disguise—
it bends the truth, it magnifies lies.
Not every thought deserves my trust,
not every worry should weigh this much.

So I let it linger, but not take control,
I hear its whispers, but don't let them grow.
It may walk beside me, but I choose the view—
Anxiety stays, but I walk through.

5. The Only Time We've Got

The clock won't ask if you're ready to start,
It won't slow down for a broken heart.
It won't wait for permission, won't bargain or bend—
Each second arrives, each second will end

Some days, it's a friend, walking beside,
Other days, a thief with nowhere to hide.
But time never waits, it won't rewind,
The past is a shadow, not something to find.

Regret looks back, rewriting the past,
Nostalgia holds on, making moments last.
Yet neither can change what's slipping away,
The only time we have is today.

So waste it, chase it, love it, let go,
Stand still or run—just live as you go.
For whether it's golden or whether it's not,
It's the only time that we have got.

6. The Child Within

From the outside, I stand tall, composed,
A mind that questions, a face that knows.
Measured words, a steady gaze,
A thinker lost in life's grand maze.

But inside—oh, inside, I'm small,
A child still chasing dreams too tall.
Building castles in thin air,
Believing life is always fair.

I build up my world with wisdom and rules,
Yet secretly dance to the songs of fools.
For reason may guide, but it cannot replace
The thrill of a heart still lost in its chase.

So let me be both—the wise and the wild,
A mind that has aged, a soul still a child.
For what is a life if not this collision—
Of knowledge hard-earned and sweet delusion?

7. The Road to Myself

I thought one day, I'd figure it out—
Who I am, what life's about.
As if the road would simply show,
A single path, a place to go.

But every time I reached a door,
I'd step inside and not be sure.
The walls would change, the floor would shake,
And once again, I'd recreate.

Some days, I swore I had it right,
Who I was in perfect sight.
But just as I held it, just as it stayed,
Life would whisper—not yet, change.

I have been the dreamer, the lost, the found,
The runner, the watcher, the one who drowns.
The one who swears they've seen the light,
Only to question it by night.

No end, no map, no final key,
No single version meant to be.
We are not answers, set in stone—
We are stories still being told.

And maybe the goal was never to find,
But to become, a little each time.
For in the searching, in the roam,
I learn that I am both path and home.